Girl at Mongar Tsechu

Boys below Wangdi Dzong

The Magic of
Gross National Happiness

*"If you see someone without a smile,
give them one of yours."*

— Robert Kenyon

The Magic of
Gross National Happiness

Doris Lee McCoy, Ph.D.

American Spirit Publishing
La Jolla, CA

DEDICATIONS

The Queen of Bhutan Ashi Dorji Wangmo Wangchuck for her strong gentleness. She founded the Tarayana Foundation which works with isolated village people of Bhutan to help them to be more productive in selling their goods and becoming literate.

The happy people of Bhutan and to those who study happiness, enabling the rest of the world to learn about those traits which encourage happiness.

Dr. Barbara Warren and Angelica Drake, world class athletes who adventured through Bhutan with a great deal of enthusiasm and provided joy to the rest of us.

ACKNOWLEDGEMENTS

The Fourth King, Jigme Singye Wangchuck, who gave me a letter giving me permission to interview any member of his cabinet,

Foreign Secretary Daw Penjo and assistant Karma Tshorar for submitting interview requests,

Ambassador Lhatu Wangchuck and Prime Minister Jigmi Thinley of the Kingdom of Bhutan for their generous help,

Dorji Penjore, Senior Researcher at the Center for Bhutan Studies for his interview,

Kinley Zam and her relatives who extended their hospitality and home, making it possible for me to participate as a member of their family,

Anna Di Bella for her wise counsel,

Lalida Sritanyaratana and Andrew Garofalo for their research, editing, and technical support,

Photographs by Karina Moreton, Panoramic Journeys and Dr. McCoy.

The Magic of Gross National Happiness

Happiness is one of those words we often toss about casually, but when did you last think very seriously about what that means to you? When do you feel happy? It seems like a simple question, but think about it more deeply. Is it when someone gives you a compliment that enables you to experience joy? Is it when you're doing your work or daily crafts and you feel intuitively that it was well done? Is it when your family is gathered around you? Is it at the dinner table? Is it when you're writing an article, a poem, shaping a piece of sculpture, or when someone who is not usually complimentary compliments you? How does your whole body feel? Relaxed?

The Merriam-Webster Dictionary defines happiness as "the quality or state of being happy; good fortune; pleasure; contentment; joy."

Wikipedia.org has a more comprehensive view of happiness. Philosophers and religious thinkers sometimes define happiness not as a state of emotional well-being, but in terms of living a good life or flourishing. Contemporary researchers have even developed tools such as *The Oxford Happiness Questionnaire*. This survey and others like it generally use theoretical models that include describing happiness as consisting of positive emotions and positive activities. Research on happiness has identified a number of attributes that correlate with happiness: positive relationships and social interaction, extraversion, marital status, satisfying employment, health, democratic freedom, optimism, religious involvement, income and proximity to other happy people.

There are many who have attempted to define happiness in previous centuries. The great Aristotle noted that "Happiness is the meaning and the purpose of life, the whole aim and end of human existence." Definitions have continued in modern times.

Mahatma Gandhi said, "Happiness is when what you think, what you say, and what you do are in harmony."

Ayn Rand said, "Happiness is that state of consciousness which proceeds from the achievement of one's values."

In levity Oscar Levant said, "Happiness is not something you experience, it's something you remember."

Ghandi's description is perhaps more definitive because he tells us most clearly how we can be most happy. Ayn Rand says we are most happy when we realize our values. When this occurs we arrive at a state of consciousness which, of course, makes us happy. What was said by Oscar Levant is simply that the joyful remembrances of things past invoke feelings of happy times, strengthening our sense of contentment and, therefore, happiness. You might note that most of the definitions do not define the actual means to achieve happiness.

All of my life I have heard people question: What actually is happiness? Most recently I have found myself asking this very same question.

Scientists, doctors, and our own institutions push us to answer this question. When one is diagnosed with cancer or other serious illnesses, our attitude scores high in the healing process. So why not look at what makes you happy every day?

Some of my Explorer Club Members just laughed when I told them of my interest in searching out the research on Gross National Happiness. They said, "There is no way you can possibly evaluate happiness." News commentators have often thought that the concept is a complete joke. So I started to ask myself the question, **"How can you evaluate happiness and how does it begin in one's life?"**

As a psychologist, I had spent many hours with parents who wanted to do the best for their children. I had been asked many times, "Are children born happy or is there something that parents can do to nurture and encourage them during the early years when they are growing up?" I had some strong feelings about this but wanted to evaluate them more closely.

Worldwide Research on Happiness

Numerous surveys suggest that Denmark is the happiest place on earth. Adrian Wright, a psychologist at the University of Leicester in the United Kingdom, compiled and analyzed data from 100 different worldwide studies on happiness. The studies surveyed over 80,000 people worldwide and placed Denmark as the happiest country in the world, with the United States ranking 23rd, Germany at 35th and England at 41st.

Another happiness research project, the World Database of Happiness, was created by Ruut Veenhoven at Erasmus University Rotterdam in the Netherlands. This study asked people to rank their life satisfaction on a scale of one through ten. In the 2008 study, again the Danes scored high and had a mean life satisfaction ranking of 8.03, compared to Americans at 7.47.

In Denmark, there is less of an emphasis placed on the correlation between income and status. The high taxes which are paid in Denmark are utilized to raise the standard of living for all, and it is believed that there is less social and economic pressure to "keep up with the Joneses." One Danish garbage man, when interviewed by *ABC News* in 2007, ranked his level of happiness at eight out of ten. He disclosed that in his country no one judges his career choice and that he enjoys his schedule—he works five hours in the morning and has the rest of the day to spend time with his family and coach his daughter's handball team.

Although there are reasons to be skeptical, researchers at the University of Southern Denmark in Odense have studied possible explanations for the supposedly high levels of happiness in Denmark. Here is what they found:

WHAT MAKES A DANE HAPPY?

Dr. Kaare Christensen, a Danish researcher wrote a paper entitled *Why Danes Are Smug: Comparative Study of Life Satisfaction in the European Union*[1] and uncovered that Danes tend to have lower expectations about the future than other countries. This, he argues, may allow Danes to be pleasantly surprised, and thus happier, when they succeed beyond their expectations. So let's look further.

- The study found that Danes eat a lot of comfort food like pasta and stew. Such foods may give them a sense of comfort and happiness.

- There is not a great disparity of wealth in Denmark.

- Danes receive benefits such as child care and provisions for higher education, for which they are paid.

- Denmark is a welfare state. By some indications they are taken care of from the crib to the crypt.

- All Danes get six weeks of vacation giving them more time to be with their families.

- One researcher suggested that "Blondes have more fun!" We may remember that many Danes are blonde.

---

[1] http://www.bmj.com/cgi/content/full/333/7582/1289, 2008

Here is what Dr. Christensen said about Americans:

AMERICANS THINK MORE IS BETTER

- Americans want it all.
- Americans nationwide often use the lifestyle and the high levels of energy and happiness in New York City as a measuring stick for their own happiness.

Are Americans happy? Disneyland claims to be "The Happiest on Earth." No doubt some children do believe that is a fact. But is that true or just an advertisement for kids to get their parents to take them to that fun Walt Disney attraction? Now let's look at happiness in a more analytical way—what does it mean?

One survey suggested that Iceland is the happiest place on earth. Perhaps it is because they are often in a cold climate and gather together to keep warm.

My enthusiasm for more information led me to seek studies that may have been done globally. In spite of all the research studies I had looked into, I had read some literature that claimed that the Kingdom of Bhutan was the happiest place on earth, so that sounded like a good place to begin my research.

I had been to the Kingdom two years before with five friends and realized there was something special about these wonderful Bhutanese people. They were kind, polite, and went to great lengths to help answer your questions. Their houses were all similar in architecture with cut-out pieces of wood adorning each structure. Perhaps this sameness pleases them.

When we visited, it was September, the time when they celebrate one of their main festivals, the Thimphu Tsechu. The festival was dedicated to Guru Rinpoche, the saint who brought Buddhism to Bhutan. (Vajrayan Buddhism is Bhutan's main religion and a major part of the fabric of its society. The country's philosophy of Gross National Happiness is woven into this fabric.) The array of colorful outfits was breathtaking. Women wore long skirts with a silk blouse and jacket. Their choice of color ranged from soft pastel shades to dark, bold, solid colors. The men followed the manner of their 14th century ancestors, wearing white undershirt cuffs turned back over their jacket sleeves, making the white cuffs four inches long.

I was very much taken by the smiling faces around me and I commented on a particularly stunning outfit worn by a local middle school teacher, who turned out to be Kinley Zam. She and I quickly became friends. The next day she found me in a handicraft store and presented me with a traditional full three-piece outfit. I was astonished with this incredible gift, but she explained that she was enthusiastic about the new book I was writing, *VISIONARIES CHANGE THE WORLD,* and she disclosed that she admired what I was accomplishing in my life.

When I returned home to America, Kinley Zam and I started to communicate by e-mail. She later invited me to visit her in her home in the capital city of Thimphu. I was pleased because this would give me not only an intellectual, outsider assessment of the culture, but would allow me to get to know the Bhutanese on a personal basis. Kinley has become instrumental in my learning the background and the concepts of Gross National Happiness.

Secretary General Chime P. Wangdi of Taryana

Dasho Sangay Wangchuck, Priry Council

The Kingdom of Bhutan is located high in the eastern Himalayas bordering on India, Nepal and China, all of which are much larger than this country that has fewer than 700,000 people. It is sometimes referred to as the last Shangri-la. "It's a magical country," I was told by Marilyn Tam, former business executive of Nike and Reebok, and now President of the US Foundation, who visits Bhutan often. Explorers Club member Brian P. Hanson, a widely traveled man said, "You have got to go back to Bhutan. You must know by now there is no other place like it in the world." I felt that to be true.

The 4th King of Bhutan, Jigme Singye Wangchuck, introduced the concept of Gross National Happiness in 1973 when the country was still under an absolute monarchy. In addition to transforming the country into a constitutional monarchy, the King developed a modernization plan that emphasized the importance of making critical economic advancements while still maintaining the emotional well-being of the people.

For years the Bhutanese were isolated. Not until recently were they open to outsiders. When I decided to go it was not easy to get a visa. I was helped by the Ambassador from Bhutan at their UN office in New York City. After sending a letter requesting an interview with the 4th King Jigme Singye Wangchuck, I received a letter telling me that I could have the opportunity to talk with any member of his cabinet. It was then that I moved forward with my travel plans.

One arrives in this country by way of the only airline they have called Druk Airlines. As we approached Mount Everest, the pilot announced that we would be able to see it on the right hand side of the plane. Everybody on the plane moved to the right and I wondered if we might just tip over in that direction because of all the excitement about seeing the world's largest mountain. I'm sure it is the closest I will ever get to it because I am primarily a rainforest explorer. My good friend and Explorers Club member Sir Edmund Hillary and Tenzing Norgay were the very first people to reach the peak. Looking down from the plane, it was obvious how difficult that climb must have been. The English had sponsored treks up to Everest for thirty-one years before Hillary reached the top.

A short time later we arrived at the Kingdom of Bhutan. Coming into their only airport in Paro is quite a thrill. Seventy-two percent of the land is covered by trees, which, worldwide, is an environmentalist's dream. Before landing, the plane has to tilt its wings slightly from side to side as it drops down into this narrow opening that finally turns into a flat air strip close to the town of Paro.

My friend Kinley greets me as I pass through customs and we begin the one-hour drive to Thimphu on winding mountain roads. The beautiful country of Bhutan engages its visitors to miles of pastoral views. The hillsides are covered with many colorful waving prayer flags that are connected together with a cord. It brought me to a sudden realization that I was in a very different country from America. Many flags are hung over areas that are difficult to reach and I wondered how they were able put them at such heights.

When we arrived at my friend Kinley's house, I was delighted to see that her family had increased. I was greeted by a grinning baby and his father who was holding, playing with, and gently rocking his son to sleep. The baby purred in response to this attention. Holding this baby happened very often in the Zam household when a teenage cousin or neighbor stopped by to visit. Anyone visiting picked up and talked to the eight-month old baby boy. It was obvious that he was loved by many and never seemed to be bothered by different people attending to or holding him. It seemed he found this to be quite normal and enjoyed the attention.

I remained with the family for three weeks, which gave me the opportunity to experience why Bhutan is called *The Happiest Place on Earth*. Children there are adored and cared for by each and everyone in the child's environment. Both mother and father feed the child and continue attending to their infant while neighbors join them. What I noticed was that the child's favorite response was always a smile. I was surprised to see that he was not frightened or teary-eyed at all. Strangers seemed to care for him in a loving way as his own parents did.

Kinley Zam

Mother and child in the street in the capital city

When I first arrived in the capital city of Thimphu I noticed something unusual, and while walking down the main street in town a few experiences alerted me to the differences between Bhutan and other places in the world. I often noticed younger children walking hand-in-hand with their mothers or fathers on their way to school. Even teenagers took the hands of younger children and walked them across the street. There was no reluctance or embarrassment in spite of their age differences. To an outsider, it was obvious that there was a strong connectedness and caring for other people. Family seemed to be very important, a pattern that I would continue to see expressed in many ways as I spent time in this Himalayan culture.

People in the village are very kind and seemed to have a welcoming attitude, even to strangers. I was trying to find a particular address and one young man, seeing my dilemma, walked me fifteen minutes to my destination. I was surprised that one person would go this far out of his way to help a visitor. Certainly there are such good Samaritans in our own country and in other parts of the world, but in Bhutan this appears to be the norm. It seems truly to be a country of helping hands.

On a trip to Kinley's Middle School

The children had a contest for the best planted garden.
It was clear how happy they were with their accomplishment.
Many who taught at the school and those who visited
stated that the garden made them happy.

Students line up for their school announcements. A close look at the photograph shows how all the students cross their arms behind them. This is different from our country, where children usually line up with their arms at their sides.

Two children in the street in Thimphu

The next day, I went to see Foreign Secretary Daw Penjo at the Ministry of Foreign Affairs. We discussed the people who might help me to know more about the Bhutanese culture and who could steer me directly to vitalize my research about Gross National Happiness (GNH). With the assistance of Karma, who was Mr. Penjo's personal assistant, I watched as he sent out my interview requests to those who specifically could help me with my project. I was told by Mr. Penjo and Karma that Susan Andrews of Brazil, who had recently visited Bhutan and would direct the 5th GNH conference, claimed that her countrymen and women felt they were very happy and shared similar traits as the people of Bhutan.

Doris Lee and Bhutanese UN Ambassador Daw Penjo,
presently Foreign Secretary.

The goal of my research was to collect and perhaps synthesize information, to bring back the fruits of my research to help Americans and others further understand the concepts of Gross National Happiness which might be implemented in their daily lives.

Bhutan has a system for gauging happiness in three main categories: very happy, happy, and not very happy. This is also broken down into rural and urban areas. I discovered this system through Lily Wangchhuk's book, *Facts About Bhutan*, which shows how happy people are in different parts of the country. In the survey, it shows how many of the people are happy with an extremely small segment of the population expressing low happiness.[2]

During my stay I experienced an extended family structure in several of the homes I visited. It appeared that within such families, individuals were respected for their personal contributions to the family. The model for a family is not necessarily enforced by the culture.

Some have suggested that India's family system could serve as a prototype for Bhutan. Although India has an extended family structure, many in Bhutan felt that it would not be the best system because many families in India live under one roof. A dominant mother often is in charge of assigning household tasks with an iron hand. It appears that this would be contrary to the Bhutanese way of life.

---

[2] Images from *Facts About Bhutan* by Lily Wangchuck

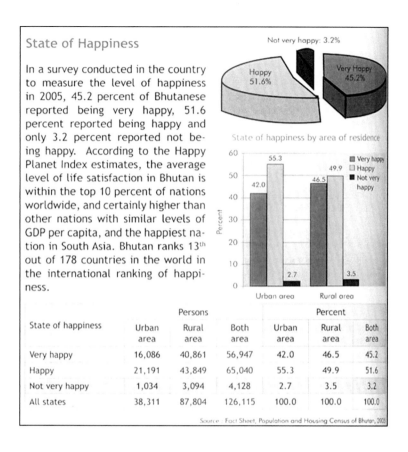

State of Happiness

In a survey conducted in the country to measure the level of happiness in 2005, 45.2 percent of Bhutanese reported being very happy, 51.6 percent reported being happy and only 3.2 percent reported not being happy. According to the Happy Planet Index estimates, the average level of life satisfaction in Bhutan is within the top 10 percent of nations worldwide, and certainly higher than other nations with similar levels of GDP per capita, and the happiest nation in South Asia. Bhutan ranks 13th out of 178 countries in the world in the international ranking of happiness.

Not very happy: 3.2%

Very Happy 45.2%

Happy 51.6%

State of happiness by area of residence

State of happiness	Persons			Percent		
	Urban area	Rural area	Both area	Urban area	Rural area	Both area
Very happy	16,086	40,861	56,947	42.0	46.5	45.2
Happy	21,191	43,849	65,040	55.3	49.9	51.6
Not very happy	1,034	3,094	4,128	2.7	3.5	3.2
All states	38,311	87,804	126,115	100.0	100.0	100.0

Source : Fact Sheet, Population and Housing Census of Bhutan, 2005

In Bhutan, a person is important not just for his financial assets as in many countries that evaluate Gross National Product (GNP). Rather, an individual is appreciated for many other personal traits.

The Centre for Bhutan Studies was my first official meeting and is the location for constant study of change. Dorji Penjore was the first Senior Researcher that I talked with. "The first phase of GNH is not like Gross National Product," he said. "GNP focuses more on monetary success but GNH stresses how happy individual people are." The famous Four Pillars of Happiness were set by the 4th King in 1974:

1) Balanced and Sustainable Development
2) Concern for Environment
3) The Importance of Continuing their Culture
4) Good Governance

As I continued my education I learned from my interviews and my mentors that there are now nine pillars, presently called Domains, with five more having been added to the original list. Some are conventional and some are nonconventional. The Nine Domains are

1) Good Governance
2) Education
3) Health
4) Concern for Environment
5) Living Standards
6) Time-use
7) The Importance of Continuing their Culture
8) Community Vitality
9) Psychological Well-being

An examination of the survey of domains provides an overview of how each domain impacts upon the philosophic purpose of improving the lives of the Bhutanese people and strengthening and integrating the overall progress of Gross National Happiness in all aspects of their lives.

1) **Good Governance:** Bhutan's Gross National Happiness website states that government "must strive to promote and strengthen competent bureaucracy, sound policies and legislation, independent judiciary and media." Furthermore, good governance means that the government's primary purpose is to bring happiness to the greatest number of people. The four basic dimensions of this domain are promoting effective government, fostering a democratic culture and trust in leaders, and fighting corruption.

2) **Education:** This domain includes an indicator study that attempts to assess the base of knowledge of the general population outside of traditional indicators. The survey assesses knowledge in thirteen arts and crafts that have not been included in other educational studies. Additionally, the survey also seeks to judge educational inequalities among different demographic groups.

3) **Health:** The health domain calls for a broader study of health care in Bhutan that goes beyond conditions of mortality and morbidity. The study aims to use health indicators that are internationally comparable.

4) **Environment:** The environmental domain surveys residents about potential environmental problems affecting their community. The survey asks questions related to river and air pollution, use of pesticides, and soil erosion.

5) **Living Standards:** This domain is designed to assess economic living standards of citizens and their reported levels of happiness, using traditional measures of poverty and

income disparity. The study goes beyond this in that it also assesses "how non-cash income affects the well-being of people."

6) **Time-use:** This domain aims to assess how people balance their work with other activities like spending time with family, playing sports, or socializing. The researchers found that people who worked long hours and had a poor work-life balance were less happy.

7) **Culture:** The researchers at the Center for Bhutan Studies are concerned with how the Bhutanese are retaining their traditional culture as new ideals and norms are becoming more prevalent. This study gauges how people feel about basic cultural elements like language, sense of identity, core values and change in values, and participation in numerous cultural activities like festivals and sports.

8) **Community Vitality:** This study gauges five components of community life: giving and volunteering, social cohesion, safety, family, and duration of stay in the community. Dorji Penjore states that this domain is merely an effort to promote the volunteerism that is already a part of traditional Bhutanese culture.

9) **Psychological Well-being:** This domain attempts to assess the psychological well-being of Bhutanese citizens through four broad categories: life satisfaction, emotional well-being, spirituality and stress.

The principles of Gross National Happiness are enshrined in Bhutan's constitution. Every act of government is supposed to be in line with the values of Gross National Happiness. Dorji Penjore notes that no one in Bhutan is landless; if they do not have land, they can appeal to the King and the King grants him at least five acres of land. However, the government places restrictions on land holdings so that no individual can own more than twenty-five acres. Another interesting government regulation aimed at adhering to Gross National Happiness principles is the legal ban on billboards. This, Penjore says, is designed to create a human scale. I asked Dorji Penjore if there was one word for him to describe Gross National Happiness? He responded enthusiastically: "Balance!"

What was quite surprising to me is what Mr. Penjore said about the number of hits that the Gross National Happiness website gets each month. They have had so many college students wanting to be interns that they had to turn all of them down. They cannot handle any more call-ins so they requested that those interested visit their website: BhutanStudies.org.bt.

The country of Bhutan is interested, at this time, in disseminating information about the happiness in Bhutan and how it affects the people of their country. An immediate goal is to reach out to universities and institutions in other parts of the world to deliver the message of Gross National Happiness. Such outreach programming finds a voice at Boston University (Boston, Massachusetts, USA), which is presently planning courses that will address the traits of Gross National Happiness.

It is hoped that this present outreach programming at Boston University will eventually impact other regions in the world. Though the university is presently concentrating on the traits of GNH, it is further hoped that BU and other educational institutions will eventually teach the philosophy and all of the concepts of Gross National Happiness.

The use of the internet has served the people of Bhutan to publicize their way of life. There are presently websites that offer information about Bhutanese affairs.

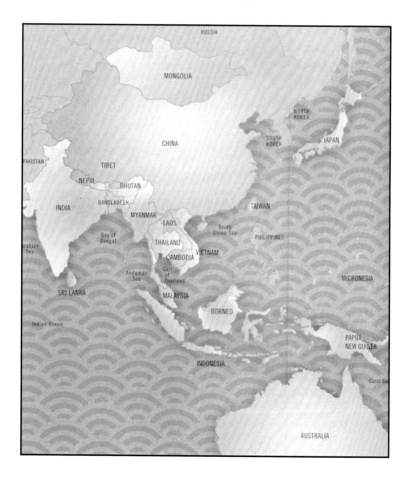

A Global Projection of Subjective Well-being:
The First Published Map of World Happiness

Map created by Adrian White, Analytic Social Psychologist, University of Leicester (2006)

Map and further analysis incorporates data published by UNESCO, the WHO, the New Economics Foundation, the Veenhoven Database, the Latinbarometer, the Afrobarometer, the CIA, and the UN Human Development Report.

Cartographic Unit · University of Leicester

Happy ———— Average ———— Unhappy

PREVIOUS WORLDWIDE CONFERENCES ON GROSS NATIONAL HAPPINESS

The following list shows how GNH has been of interest to the rest of the world. Here is an account of the conferences that have taken place to date, showing a great growth of interest in this concept.

- In 2003, the **1st International Conference on GNH** was held in Thimphu, Bhutan with 100 people attending from 18 countries.

Following the first conference, the concept of GNH picked up momentum and numerous conferences soon followed.

- **The 2nd Conference** took place in Nova Scotia, Canada from June 20 to 24, 2005 with 450 representatives from 33 countries.
- **The 3rd Conference** was in Bangkok, Thailand which attracted 800 participants from 36 countries.
- **The 4th International Conference** was held in Bhutan's capital, Thimphu, from November 25-27, 2008 with 90 participants from 25 different countries.
- **The 5th Conference** was in Brazil on November 20-24, 2009.

At the 5th Gross National Happiness conference in Brazil, over 800 policy makers, academics and business leaders discussed a variety of ways in which the principles of GNH might be implemented effectively. Brazil has been at the forefront of implementation, both in the public and private sectors. Brazilian municipalities have translated the nine domains of GNH into public policy, conducting surveys to reinforce and gain more knowledge about peoples' priorities and funding programs to address future concerns. The success of the first five conferences has provided many across the world with a sense of commitment to the philosophy of Gross National Happiness. It is anticipated that the growing "center of concern" to a philosophy which embodies a sense of well-being for all members in a community working together will provide greater interest in future conferences. The people of Bhutan have paved the way and it appears that it will not only be a Buddhist way, but a prospective philosophy for people all over the world.

A foremost leader in popularizing GNH, Dr. Susan Andrews has created the Future Vision Eco-village in Brazil, a community that incorporates sustainable environmental practices in development. The eco-village includes the principles of GNH in Brazil's educational curriculum. The idea is to produce and consume goods locally to minimize the ecological footprint. The eco-village focuses on creating stability in families, encouraging participatory government, and providing a sense of meaning in life in a beautiful environment.

Susan Andrews is of the opinion that eco-villages will offer a prototype for the GNH philosophy to become even more popular in other parts of the world. It is her hope that it will offer people an opportunity to escape the fear and anxiety of urban areas by creating places where individuals can experience the beauty of the natural landscape. The eco-villages have been successful in Brazil because eighty-five percent of the people currently live in highly urbanized areas with high levels of crime and would, therefore, benefit by such philosophical change.

Natura, a cosmetic company in Brazil, is a leader in implementing GNH principles in a business setting. The company has introduced wellness programs that include "meditation, deep dialogue, systemic thinking, and dealing with stress and time-use problems"[3].

---

[3] Choden, Phuntsho. Kuensel Newspaper, *Kids are key to success story.* 12-3-09.

Upon returning, Prime Minister Lyonchhoen Jigmi Y Thinley of Bhutan recognized that "GNH is being implemented by Non Governmental Organizations, businesses and local governments in certain parts of Brazil, which is far beyond what Bhutan is actually doing or has achieved"[4]. He added that the Bhutanese now know that they must take more steps to creatively implement GNH. He is bold in his approach with the hope of attracting followers. The Bhutanese delegation decided to form a group that will discuss how to implement GNH at the community and institutional levels in Bhutan.

Earlier, Bhutan was featured in a *New York Times* article with respect to the current economic crisis. The article, entitled "Recalculating Happiness in a Himalayan Kingdom,"[5] explored how Gross National Happiness really works.

"If the rest of the world cannot get it right in these unhappy times, this tiny Buddhist Kingdom high in the Himalayan mountains says it is working on an answer."

"Greed, insatiable human greed," said Prime Minister Jigmi Thinley of Bhutan, describing what he sees as the cause of today's economic catastrophe in the world beyond the snow-topped mountains. "What we need is change," he said in the whitewashed fortress where he works. "We need to think Gross National Happiness."

---

[4] Choden, Phuntsho. Kuensel Newspaper, *Bhutan is Falling Behind.* 11-30-09.
[5] Mydans, Seth. New York Times, *Recalculating Happiness in a Himalayan Kingdom.* 5-6-09.

"The Bhutanese are refining the country's guiding philosophy into what they see as a new political science, and it has ripened into government policy just when the world may need it", said Kinley Dorji, Secretary of Information and Communications.

The goal is not happiness itself, the prime minister explained, a concept that each person must define for himself. Rather, the government aims to create the conditions for what he called, in an updated version of the American Declaration of Independence, "the pursuit of Gross National Happiness."

Mr. Kinley Dorji said, "They resonate well, democracy and Gross National Happiness. Both place responsibility on the individual. Happiness is an individual pursuit and democracy is the empowerment of the individual."

The Bhutanese concede that if the world is to take Gross National Happiness seriously, they must work out a scheme of definitions and standards that can be quantified and measured by the big players of the world's economy.

The Bhutanese produced an intricate model of well-being that features the four Pillars, the nine Domains, and the seventy-two Indicators of Happiness.

"Specifically, the government has determined that the four Pillars of a happy society involve the balanced and sustainable development, culture, the environment and good governance. It breaks these into nine Domains: psychological well-being, ecology, health, education, culture, living standards, time-use, community vitality and good governance."

"Every two years, these indicators are to be reassessed through a nationwide questionnaire," said Karma Tshiteem, Secretary of the Gross National Happiness Commission, as he sat in his office at the end of a hard day of work that he said made him happy.

Can a country so long isolated continue its culture? Although the traditional outfits still prevail, there has been an interest in Westernization in Bhutan and it is not unusual to see Western blue jeans. The code for house building has not changed, although people are now hiring individuals to build their homes. In small villages outside of the big cities, the villagers continue to help one another in building their homes.

Television has captured the attention of many in Bhutan. They often watch it mesmerized for hours. Wrestling on television, unfortunately, has encouraged a less peaceful atmosphere. When I asked a lecturer what he felt television had contributed to his country, he said, "I guess we know how to play soccer better."

As this small formerly closed Kingdom is opened to the outside world, it is apparent that Bhutan is challenged to preserve its identity and culture.

Her Majesty the Queen Ashi Dorji Wangmo Wangchuck and Doris Lee McCoy
standing in front of her residence

Her Majesty the Queen Ashi Dorji Wangmo Wangchuck
with Doris Lee McCoy sitting in the living room of her residence

Lily Wangchhuk, author of *Facts About Bhutan, The Land of the Thunder Dragon*

Sharing stories and tea with a local Bhutanese Woman

Temple by Bhutanese craftsmen at Smithsonian Institute

Bhutan chosen as Country of the Year by Smithsonian Institute

Doris Lee at Tiger's Nest

Oprah's Magazine Goes to Bhutan

Several generations of Kinley's family,
some in Westernized dress.

Doris Lee is interviewed twice by the BBS,
the only TV station in Bhutan.

Many changes have occurred since 1999 when television was first permitted into the country. The Smithsonian Institute honored Bhutan as Country of the Year for its annual festival.

Kingdom of Bhutan Government Buildings

In the above photo, there are three tall buildings which serve as a background for rice fields. The tallest and largest is the building where the national offices and administration of the country reside. This building would be comparable to America's Capitol. The two other buildings house religious offices. It is quite obvious to one visiting these offices that in Bhutan there is no separation of church and state.

My opportunity to meet some members of the Royal Family was certainly a pleasant experience. My first meeting with Prince Jigyel Ugyen Wangchuck of Bhutan was on the occasion when he was representing his country at the Smithsonian Folklife Festival in 2008 in Washington D.C. He was asked to speak and as he approached the podium the audience seemed to appreciate his colorful outfit, a reproduction from a 14th century costume. The audience was most attracted to his colorful hand-painted boots. After the Prince, Michael Coates of NASA, the next speaker, strode to the platform with his very big lizard cowboy boots quite visible. He stood at the podium, hesitated for a minute, turned and looked at Prince Jigyel and said, "This is the first time that anyone has out-booted me." The audience responded with a great deal of laughter.

Prince Jigyel Ugyen Wangchuck of Bhutan,
Michael Coates of NASA

Doris Lee with Prince Jigyel Ugyen Wangchuck

The prince kindly agreed to be interviewed but he was soon taken away by his official duties. I did however, have an opportunity to give him a book for him to take back to his father, the fourth King. I remembered that the King admired Abraham Lincoln, and I thought that he would enjoy *Happy Birthday, Mr. Lincoln: A Commemorative Collage* by Pen Women Press of the National League of American Pen Women, a women's arts organization with administrative offices in Washington, D.C..

Revisiting Bhutan, I had the opportunity to meet with the Prince again and he took me to lunch in Thimphu. The Prince is a very amiable person with a quick and easy smile. We covered many interesting topics during my time with him. He is well educated and an enjoyable conversationalist. I recently read in the daily paper that the fifth King, Jigme Khesar Namgyel Wangchuck, honored Jigyel by appointing him Chairman of the Bhutanese Olympic Committee. Although there are seventeen sports featured in the Olympics, the favorite sports activity in Bhutan is archery.

Jigyel also serves on the Tarayana Board of Directors, which his mother, Queen Ashi Dorji Wangmo Wangchuck, founded. It is an organization that helps isolated villagers in a variety of ways, particularly by selling their products in a craft store on the main street in Thimphu. Once a year, they have a two-day event that takes place in the spring. Handwoven products are so popular that they are gone by the end of the first day.

Bhutanese crafts

Bhutanese women displaying their work with solar panels.

The Tarayana Foundation workers talk enthusiastically about the 25 illiterate women from small villages who were chosen to go to India. There they learned the Photovoltaic method of putting solar panels on roofs to get electricity. Dr. Shi, who invented the method, is from Shanghai and is in the book *VISIONARIES CHANGE THE WORLD.*

When they returned home 3 months later, they went to their villages where usually they went to bed at 5 o'clock because there was no longer any light. But this time the trained women put the solar panels up on the roof and for the very first time they had electricity, and what a revelation that was. They could stay up as long as they wanted to.

Although research was the focus of my trip, another great joy was to meet Queen Ashi Dorji Wangmo Wangchuck and Chime P. Wangdi, Secretary General of the Tarayana Foundation. The queen had read my new book, *VISIONARIES CHANGE THE WORLD*, in which world leaders are featured. The topics presented are human rights; food and nutrition; raising people out of poverty; environment, housing and pollution; eradicating landmines in Africa; curing diseases; law and democracy; saving at risk kids; turning prisoners, drug addicts, and prostitutes into good citizens; media; philanthropy; setting up non-profits; saving endangered species; helping Sudan and Darfur; exploration; music and laughter.

Queen Ashi Dorji Wangmo Wangchuck and Doris Lee

The Queen seemed very moved by the leaders in *VISION-ARIES* as she said, "Today is a very happy day for me since I met you, Doris. I think we need more people like you to bring a whole network of social workers like us to do our job. To bring a whole network of people who really care deeply about the world can make a real difference in uplifting life.

I think you have brought all of these people together in one goal and that is to make the world a better place for all of us. I salute you for that, Doris. You're one lady who has put a beat in my heart."

In spite of her very full and probably demanding schedule, the Queen took time to discuss the many contributions that the individual visionaries in my book have made to the world.

Meeting her and seeing her home with its artistically shaped bridge was a true pleasure. Our meeting brought me a sense of serenity and a peace which I have grown to identify with Gross National Happiness.

After taking photographs with the Queen at the front door it was time to say goodbye. I felt we had connected in a very personal way. I am very grateful for the hours spent with her and the time will be treasured. I will carry the experience always. It made me aware of how one can meet a stranger fifteen hours away and a short time later have a sincere friend for life.

The air in Bhutan with its many trees is so clear and refreshing to breathe. As I drove away through the meadow, I realized that the beauty of the landscape was filled with the wild flowers of this peaceful eastern Himalayan Kingdom of Bhutan. Saying goodbye to my friends on my last day there made me aware of how much they thought about the quality of life.

May you take away something from this small book that will help you to appreciate the special things in your life. My experiences in Bhutan were not only productive, but I gained a personal growth of individual happiness as I became immersed in Bhutan's philosophy of Gross National Happiness.

Secrets of Gross National Happiness For You To Use

1. Keep life simple.

2. Make time for family. Put them on your calendar.

3. Take time to have fun.

4. Provide health care for all members of your family.

5. Connect with the world as it is important to our emotional well-being.

6. Use incentives to help your children graduate, at least from high school.

7. Don't compare or contrast your children to others. They all have their own uniqueness.

8. Teach your children that success comes from character, not from being rich and famous.

9. Do not overly protect your children. Teach them that struggle is a way of finding out more about themselves.

10. Celebrate your cultural history, as well as the founders and creators of your country.

11. Volunteer your time. Work together as a family.

12. Surround yourself with positive people and encourage others to be positive.

13. Value frugality. Do you really need more "things"?

14. Help your neighbors who are going through hard times.

15. Don't let unnecessary things fill up your time. Be careful of the "time bandits."

16. Use your environment respectfully, preserving it for the future.

17. Make time for hobbies.

18. Respect creativity; it can heal you.

19. Learn to live happily with yourself, your family, and your community.

20. Live with balance.

Facts About Bhutan
The Land of the Thunder Dragon
by Lily Wangchhuk

General Information on Visiting Bhutan

With the exception of travelers from India, Bangladesh and Maldives, all visitors to Bhutan require a visa. Visas can only be obtained through a Bhutanese tour operator after full payment has been made. Air tickets to Bhutan can only be issued after the visa is issued. Bhutanese Embassies and Missions abroad do not issue visas for private visitors to Bhutan.

Best Times to Travel

Winter (November-January) is the best time of the year for bird watching, trekking in the lower altitudes or a bicycle trip along the mountain roads. The trekking routes in the high mountains are covered in deep snow and are impassable at this time of year. The endangered Black-necked Crane spends the winter in the high valley of Bomdeling (in eastern Bhutan) and Phobjikha (in western Bhutan).

Spring (February–April) is a perfect time for kayaking, rafting, and trekking in moderate altitudes. The most popular religious dance festival *Paro Tshechu* takes place in spring.

Summer (May-August) brings with it the monsoon, but this should not dissuade travelers. Rain falls for short periods daily but is manageable with adequate planning and equipment. Pleasant summer temperatures without heat or humidity can be found in central and western Bhutan. Treks in high mountain areas are characterized by mild temperatures and vibrant flora.

Autumn (September – October) is the traditional high season in Bhutan. September and October have the highest number of Tsechus (festivals). Trekkers particularly enjoy the clear view of the mountains in October and the low rainfall. Rice harvest means a picturesque landscape and remarkable terraces and changing colour.

To Reach Bhutan by Air

The most convenient way of entering Bhutan is by Druk Air, the national carrier which operates daily flights from Bangkok (Thailand), three times a week from Delhi, four times a week from Kolkata, once a week from Bodh Gaya (India), three times a week from Kathmandu (Nepal) and once a week from Dhaka (Bangladesh) to Paro (Bhutan). The flight timings and frequency vary according to season. The flight offers spectacular views of the Himalayan ranges including the Mount Everest region which is seen at its best during the winter months, when skies are generally very clear. The airport is about an hour drive from the capital, Thimphu.

Recreational Activities for Visitors

Cultural Tours

The cultural tours will provide visitors with a first hand experience of many aspects of Bhutanese life and culture. These tours introduce visitors to unique aspects of Bhutanese history and preserved culture with visits to 17th century Dzongs, religious dance festivals, pilgrimage sites, museums, fascinating excursions to villages and monasteries. Local sightseeing offers an insight into the distinct culture, age old traditions and the lifestyle of the deeply spiritual and mystical kingdom.

Festival

The tshechus that take place throughout the country in every Dzongkhag at different times of the year can last up to four days and are worth experiencing. The several local community festivals held in various villages throughout the country attract the local populace in a spirit of festivity, celebration and deep faith. These festivals are visually stunning and give visitors an insight into the vibrant and rich culture of the country.

Bird Watching

With an estimated 770 species and a great variety of endangered species, Bhutan is an ideal place to see a wide variety of birds that may be impossible or difficult to spot anywhere else.

Botanical Tours

With 7,000 vascular plants, 360 orchid species, 46 species of rhododendron and about 500 species of medicinal plants, Bhutan is a true haven of biodiversity for nature lovers. The beginning of the monsoon season is the best time to see the best of the country's flora, while spring is the ideal time to see the flowering rhododendrons, magnolias, and other spring flowers and shrubs.

Fishing

In a Buddhist country, fishing is not common among its people, but for visitors fishing in the crystal clear rivers set against breathtaking landscapes can be quite an experience. Fishing spots range from large rivers to crystal clear spring-fed streams at altitudes ranging from 1,200m to 3,000m. The most common varieties are snow trout and brown trout. The best times for fishing are in spring (February to April) and autumn (September to October).

Travel Tips

Communication Facilities

Reliable telephone and fax services are available in all towns in Bhutan. International connections are excellent. Internet cafes are few in number and available in only a few places. However, most tourist hotels have internet connection. A prepaid SIM card can be purchased, and you can use your mobile phones in most of the major towns in the country.

Health Information

No vaccinations are currently required for traveling to Bhutan. However, visitors coming from an area infected with yellow fever are required to get a yellow fever vaccination and it must be administered at least ten days before entry into Bhutan.

Shopping

The country's exquisite postage stamps, lovely hand woven fabrics, carved masks, woven baskets, wooden bowls, hand-made papers, finely crafted metal objects, thangkha paintings are popular items purchased by foreign visitors. Buying and selling of antiques is strictly forbidden in the kingdom.

Winding Roads

The roads are winding and narrow by western standards. Since Bhutan is a mountainous country it takes time to travel from place to place. To travel 127 km it may take 5 hours.

Clothing

While casual clothes are fine, sleeveless tops, shorts, and caps are strictly not permitted for entry into Dzongs, government offices and monastic festivals. To withstand Bhutan's changeable weather, it is advisable to bring travel clothes and warmer clothes for evenings.

Photography

Bhutan is a photographer's paradise. However, it is recommended to seek permission before you photograph people and places of interest.

Smoking in Public Places

On the 17th of December 2004, in keeping with the decision of the Bhutanese parliament, the nationwide ban on the sale of tobacco products was implemented, making Bhutan the first country in the world to do so. Smoking in public places which includes parks, discotheques, entertainment centers, sports facilities like football grounds and archery ranges, commercial centers including shops, bars and restaurants, institutions like Dzongs, hospitals, schools, and government offices, public transport carriers, public gatherings such as monastic festivals, official receptions, national celebrations, and vegetable market is banned.

Bhutan's Diplomatic Missions Abroad

United States
Permanent Mission of the Kingdom of Bhutan
to the United Nations
Two United Nations Plaza, 27th Floor, New York, NY 10017, U.S.A
Tel: (+1-212) 826-1919, 826-1990/1
Fax: (+1-212) 826-2998
Email:pmbnewyork@aol.com

Bibliography

Tenth Five Year Plan 92008-2013) Vol. 1, Main Document, GNH Commission, RGoB, February 2008

Gross National Happiness, Its Assumptions and Applications (Concept Paper), Karma Galey, 2008.

The Constitution of the Kingdom of Bhutan, Royal Government of Bhutan, 2008.

Bhutan, Information Brochure, Department of Tourism, 2007.

Bhutan, Land of the Thunder Dragon, Department of Tourism, 2007.

Immortal Lines, Speeches of the 4th Druk Gyalpo Jigme Singye Wangchuk, Bhutan Times, 2007.

Good Governance Plus, Royal Government of Bhutan, 2005.

A History of Bhutan (A supplementary text for class XI), Ministry of Education, Royal Government of Bhutan, 2005.

Bhutan, Himalayan Mountain Kingdom, Francoise Pommaret, 2005.

Window on Bhutan, Royal Bhutanese Embassy, New Delhi, 2004.

World Lonely Planet Guide to Bhutan, Stan Armington, 1998.

An Introduction to Traditional Architecture of Bhutan, Department of Works, Housing and Roads, Royal Government of Bhutan, 1993.

Our special thanks to Lily Wangchhuk for permission to use this information from her marvelous book called
Facts About Bhutan, The Land of the Thunder Dragon
Absolute Bhutan Books
(ISBN 99936-760-0-4)
Thimphu, Bhutan
Web: www.absolutebhutanbooks.com.bt
HS/TPHU/BICMA/1002

If you would like, please leave a comment on my
Facebook Fan Page entitled
The Magic of Gross National Happiness.

A Good Travel Code

*"Come to listen, not to preach. Come to witness, not to judge.
Allow their culture to make a change within you."*
— Robert Kenyon

Other Books About Gross National Happiness

Gross National Happiness: Why Happiness Matters for America—and How We Can Get More of It by Arthur C. Brooks.
ISBN: 978-0-456-00278-8

The Geography of Bliss by Eric Weiner.
ISBN: 978-0-446-58026-7

A Kid's Guide to Giving by Freddi Zeiler.
www.innovativekids.com

Facts About Bhutan by Lily Wangchhuk
ISBN: 99936-760-0-4. Email: abs@druknet.bt.
www.absolutebhutanbooks.com.bt

A Bhutanese village farm woman cooking.

About The Author

Doris Lee McCoy, Ph.D. is an Author, Interviewer, Psychologist, International Keynote Speaker, TV Moderator and Producer. She has interviewed over 3,000 successful entrepreneurs, politicians, celebrities, artists and athletes. Her first book, *MEGATRAITS: 12 Traits Of Successful People* includes interviews with: Malcolm Forbes, Supreme Court Justice Sandra Day O'Connor, Ronald Reagan, Gerald Ford, Mary Kay, Charlton Heston, Gregory Peck, Norman Lear and others. She was featured on 100+ TV and radio shows to speak about the book. Nightingale Conant and Discovery Tapes released a six-cassette audio album in conjunction with MEGATRAITS.

Dr. McCoy moderated and produced 20 television specials and 3 television series, including "THE CHANGING WOMAN" television series. They discussed the art of balancing highly successful careers with family, friends and future goals with interviewees including: First Ladies Betty Ford, Rosalynn Carter, Mrs. L.B. Johnson and Senator Edward Kennedy, Walter Cronkite and Lee Iacocca. Shown on Cox Cable stations.

In Kenya, Beijing and Mexico City, Dr. McCoy covered the International UN Conferences on Women. The Television Special, "WOMEN OF THE WORLD" featured her interviews with UN delegates from Asia, Europe, Africa and aired throughout the USA. American Airlines aired her interviews for the "This I Believe" audio-cassette series.

Her many years in television, teaching, speaking and consulting qualify her as a communications specialist. High-energy professionalism and personal warmth characterize her on and off the screen.

Whether shooting on location in the rainforest or interviewing top American executives, her crisp, energetic, "from-the-heart" flair comes through.

To have Dr. McCoy speak for your group or consult with your company, please contact:

Ph/Fax:(858)459-4971 • Email: dorisleem@gmail.com
www.dorisleemccoy.com

Spectators at Mongar Tsechu

Siblings above Trashigang